OUR
GRE★T
STATES

WHAT'S GREAT ABOUT
MICHIGAN?

✳ Anita Yasuda

LERNER PUBLICATIONS ✳ MINNEAPOLIS

CONTENTS

MICHIGAN WELCOMES YOU! ✳ 4

Content Consultant: R. D. Jones, PhD,
Department of History and Philosophy, Eastern
Michigan University

Lerner Publications Company
A division of Lerner Publishing Group, Inc.
241 First Avenue North
Minneapolis, MN 55401 USA

For reading levels and more information, look
up this title at www.lernerbooks.com.

Main body text set in ITC Franklin Gothic Std
Book Condensed 12/15.
Typeface provided by Adobe Systems.

Library of Congress Cataloging-in-Publication
Data

Yasuda, Anita.
    What's great about Michigan? / by
Anita Yasuda.
        pages cm. — (Our great states)
    Includes index.
    Audience: Grades K–3.
    ISBN 978-1-4677-3886-6 (lb : alk.
paper) — ISBN 978-1-4677-8507-5 (pb :
alk. paper) — ISBN 978-1-4677-8508-2
(eb pdf)
    1. Michigan—Juvenile literature. I. Title.
F566.3.Y47 2016
977.4—dc23   2015000326

Manufactured in the United States of America
1 - PC – 7/15/15

MICHIGAN Welcomes You!

Michigan is filled with adventures all year round. Four giant freshwater lakes hug its borders. The Great Lakes are perfect for swimming or boating! Miles of trails and rivers wind through forests. This state has more than two hundred waterfalls to explore. You and a friend can race down Sleeping Bear Dunes National Lakeshore in the summer. There are giant hills of sand! Go to Comerica Park to cheer on the Detroit Tigers baseball team. In the winter, you can toboggan down snowy slopes in Muskegon or ice-skate on outdoor rinks. There are always fun things to see and do in the Great Lake State. Keep reading to learn about ten places that make Michigan great!

Explore Michigan's cities and all the places in between! Just turn the page to find out all about the GREAT LAKE STATE. >

Mount Arvon
(1,979 feet/603 m)

LAKE SUPERIOR

CANADA

UPPER PENINSULA

Mackinac
Island

Miles
0   20   40   60
0   40   80
Kilometers

WISCONSIN

LAKE MICHIGAN

LAKE HURON

N

CANADA

Grand
Rapids

Grand   River

Flint

Lansing

Sterling
Heights

Grand Haven

Kalamazoo

Warren

Livonia

Westland

River

Ann Arbor

Dearborn

Detroit

Detroit River

ILLINOIS

INDIANA

OHIO

LAKE
ERIE

NORTHERN MICHIGAN

> Begin your Michigan adventure in Mackinaw City. Investigate the state's past at Colonial Michilimackinac on the shores of Lake Michigan. Costumed guides make this fort and fur-trading village from the 1700s come to life. And you can be part of history! Put on a redcoat uniform and become a British soldier. After you have finished your drills, join a game of lacrosse. Or dance at a colonial wedding. Then become a French trader. See what you can get for your pelts.

Take the ferry across the lake to explore Mackinac Island. No cars are allowed on the island. You can rent a bike or go on a horse-drawn carriage tour. You'll see some of the island's natural wonders. Climb Arch Rock. It rises nearly fifteen stories into the air! From the top, you can see Canada and Lake Huron.

Later, visit the Wings of Mackinac. This building is home to hundreds of butterflies. How many different kinds can you spot? One may hitch a ride on you!

Dress up as French fur traders at Colonial Michilimackinac.

PENINSULAS

In 1833, Michigan territory wanted to become a state. At the time, Michigan and Ohio were arguing over a small piece of land on their border. Michigan had to reach an agreement with Ohio before it would be granted statehood. In the compromise, Ohio received this land while Michigan gained the western part of the Upper Peninsula north of Lake Michigan. This is how Michigan became the only state divided into two peninsulas. Michigan officially became a state in 1837.

DUTCH VILLAGE

> Do you see a sea of tulips and a large windmill? You must be at Nelis' Dutch Village in Holland—Holland, Michigan, that is! You'll think you are in Europe when you're greeted with a friendly dance. Dutch dancers wear baggy pants and wooden shoes to dance the "Welkom." See how the wooden shoes are made. Try them on. Wooden shoes can be comfortable!

Run to a slide shaped like a giant shoe. You can slide down from the heel. Be certain to go on a guided tour of the Dutch windmill. It was shipped from the Netherlands. Then soar on the swings. You can even learn a few Dutch phrases, race rubber ducks, or run through a Gouda cheese maze.

Become an honorary Dutch dancer for the day in your wooden shoes.

See many different windmills while walking through Nelis' Dutch Village.

Eat your cherries from the National Cherry Festival right off the tree or save them for cherry pie!

SLEEPING BEAR DUNES

> At Sleeping Bear Dunes National Lakeshore, you'll stand on giant hills of sand. The park has been named the most beautiful place in the United States. Challenge friends to a race. Who can run down the 450-foot-high (137-meter) dunes the fastest? Or maybe it would be faster to roll down! Afterward, visit the Maritime Museum in Glen Haven. You can watch an old cannon fire. The cannon shoots a rope that can be used to pull shipwreck victims out of the water.

Later, grab some cherry goodies at Cherry Republic in Glen Arbor. You can pick up all kinds of treats, from hot cherry pepper jelly to cherry soda. Everything is cherrylicious! You can continue celebrating cherries at nearby Traverse City's National Cherry Festival. Pick your own cherries at an orchard.

OJIBWE LEGEND

American Indians called the Ojibwe live in Michigan's Upper Peninsula. An Ojibwe legend tells of a mother bear and her cubs that swam across Lake Michigan to escape a forest fire. Sadly, the cubs died. But the Great Spirit covered them with sand. The mother bear lay down on the shore to wait for her cubs. She became the Sleeping Bear Dunes.

MUSKEGON

Feel your stomach drop as you race along at speeds of up to 65 miles (105 km) per hour on Shivering Timbers.

> Muskegon is a fun lakeside town with 26 miles (42 kilometers) of sandy beach. You can also visit Michigan's Adventure amusement park. This park has more than sixty rides. One is the longest and fastest wooden roller coaster in Michigan—Shivering Timbers.

Do you like to get soaked on a hot day? Cross the park to WildWater Adventure Park. Here you can stomp on jets of water in the playground. Walk the pirate's plank or face the tidal wave. Then fire cannons of water or slide down the Funnel of Fear on a four-person raft. If you dare, twist and turn down the Wild Slide. Splash!

In the winter, Muskegon Winter Sports Complex is one of the most popular resorts in Michigan. Visitors enjoy sledding, snowshoeing, and three ice-skating rinks. The resort even has a luge track. You can try this Olympic sport yourself. Lie feetfirst on a sled while racing down an icy slope!

Lace up your skates at one of Muskegon Winter Sports Complex's three ice rinks.

TAHQUAMENON FALLS
STATE PARK

> Do you hear that sound in the distance? It's the water of Tahquamenon Falls plunging over a rocky hillside. This is the tallest waterfall in the state! In the winter, the falls looks like a frozen ice sculpture. But in the summer, it is a fury of bubbles. Maybe your family will rent a canoe at the Lower Falls and head down the Tahquamenon River.

Nearby, you can watch huge freighters from all around the world sailing through the Soo Locks in Sault Ste. Marie. The locks are one of the largest sets of locks in the world. Hop aboard a sightseeing cruise along the river and through the locks. You'll be amazed as your boat is raised 21 feet (6 m) to the level of Lake Superior.

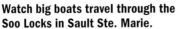

Watch big boats travel through the Soo Locks in Sault Ste. Marie.

THE FUR TRADE

French fur traders came to the area that is now Michigan around 1700. They were looking for pelts to sell in Europe. The French built forts to support the fur trade as it grew. Some forts were built near waterways. The waterways would later move goods from the country's interior to the coast. The French also built forts near American Indian villages. The French exchanged items—such as pots, knives, and guns—for pelts.

Build a bridge or launch a boat at the Great Lakes Garden.

GRAND RAPIDS

> Be sure to visit Grand Rapids! It's a city with many outdoor activities to choose from. The Frederik Meijer Gardens & Sculpture Park is a fun-filled adventure. It starts when you enter through a child-sized mouse hole! Climb into the tree house village for a great view of the park, or dig for fossils in the rock quarry. Learn more about the Great Lakes at the Great Lakes Garden. The ponds are shaped like the lakes! Then pick vegetables and feed the animals at Michigan's Farm Garden.

Want to see even more animals? Visit the John Ball Zoo. You can say hello to more than one thousand animals. Touch a stingray in Stingray Lagoon. Feed sharks or enjoy a ride on a camel. You may even get to pet a snake.

Explore the playhouses throughout the Frederik Meijer Gardens & Sculpture Park.

FRANKENMUTH

> Take a trip to the German-inspired town of Frankenmuth. Enjoy a festival, shopping, or a horse-drawn carriage ride in this quiet town. Then head to the Adventure Park. You'll lose any fear of heights you had here. There are 5 acres (2 hectares) of rope bridges, cables, and zip lines that take you high above the forest floor.

In the center of town, explore a maze with thousands of mirrors. Don't be fooled by the dead ends and circles! If you get hungry, stop by the Bavarian Inn for a meal. Learn to roll a large pretzel.

A little farther south, visit Crossroads Village in Flint. Guides dress in period clothing at this 1800s living museum. They are never out of character. Talk to the blacksmith or learn how to work the printing press. The Huckleberry Railroad train is an authentic steam locomotive. It runs daily in Crossroads Village.

Enjoy your homemade pretzel piping hot from the oven at the Bavarian Inn.

You can take a ride on the steam train at Crossroads Village.

Try feeding leaves to one of the Detroit Zoo's giraffes.

DETROIT

> Check out a Detroit Tigers baseball game at Comerica Park. Before the game, you can ride the carousel with its thirty painted tigers. Or let a baseball-shaped car on the Fly Ball Ferris Wheel carry you into the air. Visit a batting cage to test your baseball skills. Will you be drafted into the major leagues? Kids aged fourteen and under can run the bases after every Sunday game.

Next, go to the Detroit Zoo to see North America's largest polar bear exhibit. You will feel as though you have entered the North Pole. Stand in an 8-foot-tall (2 m) tunnel under the water. Polar bears and seals swim above you! And a few lucky visitors can feed the giraffes. You might think of becoming a zookeeper yourself!

MOTOWN SOUND

Motown sound was a mix of pop and soul music popular in the 1960s. Motown Records in Detroit created the genre. Each of the record company's artists had a unique sound. The music combined powerful singers, gospel, rhythm and blues, and pop music. Motown Records hoped both African American and white teenagers would dance to the music. They did—Motown sound was as popular as the Beatles. Many famous African American singers worked with Motown Records, including the Supremes, Stevie Wonder, and the Four Tops (left).

AIR ZOO

> Imagine sitting in an open cockpit and looking down at a patchwork of fields. Pilots take passengers into the sky in a real biplane at the Air Zoo in Portage. Back at the museum, grab a seat in one of several kinds of flight simulators and blast off. Special effects will make you feel as though you are navigating a space shuttle through the stars. Maybe a job at NASA is in your future! Next, take the controls of a fighter plane. Prepare for an amazing trip as you perform barrel rolls and touchdowns.

After lunch at the Kitty Hawk Cafe, ride the indoor Ferris wheel. Later, you can experience weightlessness on the Paratrooper Jump ride. It will leave you breathless!

Learn more about a NASA space shuttle's computers and controls.

Check out rides that make you feel like you are weightless at the Air Zoo!

HENRY FORD MUSEUM

Ride in a vintage Model T Ford at Greenfield Village.

> Explore new ideas at America's largest indoor-outdoor museum. Henry Ford Museum in Dearborn holds many special events throughout the year. One of these events is the Maker Faire Detroit. Here more than four hundred people show off their inventions. The event features technology, education, science, and many more subjects.

Inside the museum are many planes, trains, and cars. At the Driving America exhibit, see Theodore Roosevelt's horse-drawn carriage and other presidential vehicles. Each Saturday, the museum has interactive events. How would you like to build your own robot or launch an air rocket? Whether you ride in a giant bicycle wheel or check out the robots, fun is guaranteed.

Next door is the outdoor part of the museum. Learn about railroads, farms, and blacksmithing during the 1920s at Greenfield Village. Check out a replica of inventor Thomas Edison's lab. Talk to actors portraying historical figures such as the Wright brothers. The Wright brothers invented and built the first airplane.

YOUR TOP TEN

Now that you've read about ten awesome things to see and do in Michigan, think about what your own Michigan top ten list would include. If you were planning a Michigan vacation, what would you like to see? Write your top ten list on a separate sheet of paper or turn your list into a poster. You can add drawings or pictures from the Internet or magazines.

Visitors to the Henry Ford Museum can climb in replicas of vehicles like this bus from the 1950s.

MICHIGAN BY MAP

> MAP KEY

⊛ Capital city

○ City

◎ Point of interest

▲ Highest elevation

–··– International border

–·– State border

Visit www.lernerresource.com to learn more about the state flag of Michigan.

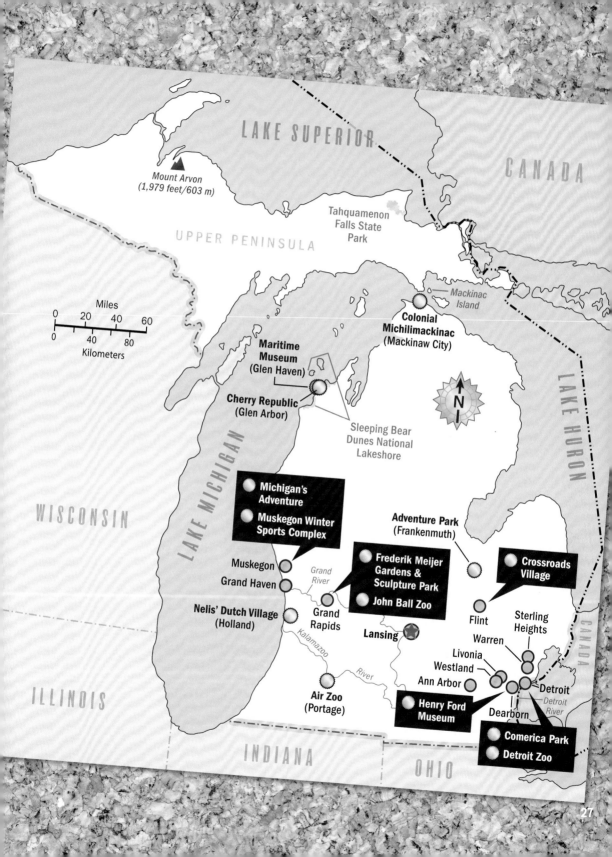

LAKE SUPERIOR

CANADA

UPPER PENINSULA

Mount Arvon
(1,979 feet/603 m)

Tahquamenon
Falls State
Park

Mackinac
Island

Colonial
Michilimackinac
(Mackinaw City)

Maritime
Museum
(Glen Haven)

Cherry Republic
(Glen Arbor)

Sleeping Bear
Dunes National
Lakeshore

N

LAKE MICHIGAN

LAKE HURON

WISCONSIN

Miles
0   20   40   60
0   40   80
Kilometers

Michigan's
Adventure

Muskegon Winter
Sports Complex

Adventure Park
(Frankenmuth)

Crossroads
Village

Muskegon

Grand Haven

Nelis' Dutch Village
(Holland)

Grand
River

Frederik Meijer
Gardens &
Sculpture Park

John Ball Zoo

Grand
Rapids

Flint

Sterling
Heights

Lansing

Warren

Livonia

Westland

Kalamazoo
River

Ann Arbor

Detroit

Air Zoo
(Portage)

Henry Ford
Museum

Dearborn

Detroit
River

Comerica Park

Detroit Zoo

CANADA

ILLINOIS

INDIANA

OHIO

MICHIGAN FACTS

NICKNAME: The Great Lake State

SONG: "My Michigan" by Giles Kavanagh and H. O'Reilly Clint

MOTTO: *Si Quaeris Peninsulam Amoenam, Circumspice,* or "If You Seek a Pleasant Peninsula, Look about You."

> FLOWER: apple blossom

TREE: Eastern white pine

> BIRD: American robin

ANIMAL: white-tailed deer

DATE AND RANK OF STATEHOOD: January 26, 1837; the 26th state

> CAPITAL: Lansing

AREA: 58,692 square miles (152,012 sq. km)

AVERAGE JANUARY TEMPERATURE: 20°F (−7°C)

AVERAGE JULY TEMPERATURE: 69°F (21°C)

POPULATION AND RANK: 9,895,622; 9th (2013)

MAJOR CITIES AND POPULATIONS: Detroit (688,701), Grand Rapids (192,294), Warren (134,873), Sterling Heights (131,224), Lansing (113,972)

NUMBER OF US CONGRESS MEMBERS: 14 representatives, 2 senators

NUMBER OF ELECTORAL VOTES: 16

NATURAL RESOURCES: iron ore, natural gas, petroleum

> AGRICULTURAL PRODUCTS: apples, beef cattle, blueberries, corn, eggs, hogs

MANUFACTURED GOODS: chemicals, fabricated metal products, food products, furniture, machinery, transportation equipment

STATE HOLIDAYS AND CELEBRATIONS: Traverse City National Cherry Festival

GLOSSARY

colonial: relating to the original thirteen colonies forming the United States

freighter: a special ship designed to carry goods

Great Lakes: a chain of five freshwater lakes on the Canadian and American border

lock: a system that lowers or raises ships between different water levels

orchard: land on which fruit trees are planted

pelt: fur that has been taken from an animal

peninsula: a piece of land that is bordered by water on three sides

redcoat: a soldier in the British army

LERNER

SOURCE™

Expand learning beyond the printed book. Download free, complementary educational resources for this book from our website, www.lerneresource.com.

FURTHER INFORMATION

A to Z Kids Stuff: Michigan
http://www.atozkidsstuff.com/mi.html
Check out this website to learn all about things to do in Michigan.

Craats, Rennay. *Michigan: The Wolverine State*. New York: AV² by Weigl, 2012.
Check out this book for more fun historical and geographical facts
about Michigan.

Michigan Kids!
http://www.michigan.gov/kids
Explore this official Michigan government site to read more about Michigan's
history, government, and geography.

Noble, Trinka Hakes. *The Legend of Michigan*. Chelsea, MI: Sleeping Bear,
2006. This retelling of a classic American Indian myth explains why Michigan
is shaped like a mitten.

Piehl, Janet. *The Great Lakes*. Minneapolis: Lerner Publications, 2010. Learn
all about the Great Lakes that border Michigan.

Pure Michigan
http://www.michigan.org
Visit Michigan's official tourism page for information on places to see, things
to do, and events.

INDEX

PHOTO ACKNOWLEDGMENTS

The images in this book are used with the permission of: © Kenneth Keifer/Shutterstock Images, p. 1; NASA, pp. 2–3; © Laura Westlund/Independent Picture Service, pp. 5 (bottom), 27; © Katherine Welles/Shutterstock Images, p. 4; © ineb1599/iStock/Thinkstock, p. 5 (top); © Blanscape/Shutterstock Images, pp. 6–7; © Beth Gauper/KRT/Newscom, p. 7 (left); © Oleksandr Koretskyi/Shutterstock Images, p. 7 (right); © LadyDragonflyCC CC 2.0, pp. 8–9; © benkrut/iStockphoto, p. 9 (top); © Randa Bishop/Danita Delimont Photography/Newscom, pp. 9 (bottom), 16–17; © Rooey202 CC 2.0, pp. 10–11; © Egor Tetiushev/Shutterstock Images, p. 10; © Dean Pennala/Shutterstock Images, p. 11; © Jeremy Thompson CC 2.0, pp. 12–13, 12; © XiXinXing/Shutterstock Images, p. 13; © Kenneth Keifer/iStockphoto, pp. 14–15; © Michelle Hill/US Army Corps of Engineers CC 2.0, p. 15 (top); © Thomas Conant, p. 15 (bottom); © Steven Depolo CC 2.0, p. 16; © Images-USA/Alamy, p. 17; © Kenneth Sponsler/Shutterstock Images, pp. 18–19; © River North Photography/iStockphoto, p. 18; © Andre Jenny Stock Connection Worldwide/Newscom, p. 19; © Steve Pepple/Shutterstock Images, pp. 20–21; © Dave Hogg CC 2.0, p. 20; © PF1 WENN Photos/Newscom, p. 21; © Michael Snell/Robert Harding/Newscom, pp. 22–23; © Michael Snell/Alamy, p. 23; © David Wilson CC 2.0, pp. 24–25; © David R. Frazier/Danita Delimont Photography/Newscom, p. 24; © J. Kyle Keener/KRT/Newscom, p. 25; © nicoolay/iStockphoto, p. 26; © Cimmerian/iStockphoto, p. 29 (top); © janeff/iStockphoto, p. 29 (middle left); © Lumigraphics/iStockphoto, p. 29 (middle right); © aluxum/iStockphoto, p. 29 (bottom).

Front cover: Joe Restuccia III/DanitaDelimont.com Danita Delimont Photography/Newscom, (Museum); © William J. Hebert, courtesy of Frederik Meijer Gardens & Sculpture Park (gardens); © Frank Pierson/flickr.com (CC BY 2.0), (butterfly); Walter Bibikow/DanitaDelimont.com Danita Delimont Photography/Newscom (Comerica Park); © Laura Westlund/Independent Picture Service (map); © iStockphoto.com/fpm (seal); © iStockphoto.com/vicm (pushpins); © iStockphoto.com/benz190 (corkboard).